70s DINNER PARTY

70s DINNER PARTY

The Good, the Bad and the Downright Ugly of Retro Food

Anna Pallai

 SQUARE PEG

1 3 5 7 9 10 8 6 4 2

Square Peg, an imprint of Vintage,
20 Vauxhall Bridge Road, London SW1V 2SA

Square Peg is part of the Penguin Random House group of companies
whose addresses can be found at global.penguinrandomhouse.com

Penguin
Random House
UK

First published by Square Peg in 2016
www.vintage-books.co.uk

A CIP catalogue record for this book is available from the British Library
ISBN 9781910931387

Designed by James Ward
Printed and bound in China by C&C Offset Printing Co Ltd

Penguin Random House is committed to a sustainable future for our
business, our readers and our planet. This book is made from Forest
Stewardship Council ® certified paper.

MIX
Paper from
responsible sources
FSC® C018179

For Mum. You're the best.

INTRODUCTION

I grew up in a house where stuffed peppers and meat loaf were a regular feature and no celebration was complete without a platter of greying boiled eggs stuffed with salad cream. The crockery was heavy and brown and the air was always thick with fag smoke.

I guess loads of people who grew up in the seventies or early eighties remember a similar sort of set-up. And mine was worse than most given that my dad was from Hungary – a land where it will forever be 1975. Our meal times in south-west London were heavily tinged with a taste of Budapest, and it was not for the weak of stomach. You know how posh people conclude their dinners with an espresso and a little Italian biscuit? In my house, we finished it the Hungarian way: with a slab of speck (basically smoked lard), a dish of raw onions and a glass of their national drink, palinka (a bit like battery acid, only fruitier). It's not that the food didn't taste nice. It was just that it looked petrifying. And eventually gave you gout. And also it didn't taste nice. I decided to save myself by going vegetarian when I was twelve.

Yes, it's safe to say that I have encountered my share of ridiculous food. My childhood dinner times were often bizarre, sometimes surreal and occasionally quite terrifying.

But many of them were memorable and remain etched upon my mind's eye. Which is good because I didn't take any actual pictures. Mostly because I was always out of film on my Kodak Ektralite – it only had ten exposures and Boots took almost a month to get the pics developed. It just didn't seem worth the hassle. I mean, who would want to see a picture of my dinner? Even if it was my mother's majestically fashioned sausage and mash cabin with frozen pea roof tiles and chipolata chimney (true story).

What's weird is that, nowadays, most people's dinners are far less interesting to look at – and yet they are far more likely to take photographs of them and force other people to look at them.

There was a time when food was food. You cooked it, you moulded it, you let it set, and then you covered it with chopped boiled egg and olives. Then you just ate the lot and tried to put the whole horrible experience behind you.

This was the era of the showboat dinner party, where the upwardly mobile British family would invite peers and colleagues into their homes in a bid to wow them via high-voltage, no holds barred, brightly coloured and utterly insane three course extravaganzas. It was a time of meals that didn't just taste great, they looked great too.

In the current climate of clean-eating, smug-looking, fitness-bragging, social media fascism, the 70s dinner party now seems to signify a happier, more honest time. There are legions of us all over the world who have been forced to look at our friend's tedious, healthy lifestyle choices and now we've had enough. We want something different, something more authentic, something with a little more soul. We want something that has the balls to be shamelessly, completely and proudly crap. We want a good, old fashioned 70s Dinner Party.

CANAPÉS

The drinks party is the roguish younger cousin of the dinner party. It's from the same high-class gene-pool but rather more likely to chuck its car keys onto the coffee table and shoot a cheeky wink at the boss' wife, Joan.

A well-organised drinks party sends friends, family and your husband's important work colleagues a clear signal that you are a hostess of class and distinction.

But be careful, it is a fine line that divides the truly sophisticated drinks soirée and a cheap booze-up. . .

What makes all the difference are your snacks. Or, as our continental cousins call them: *canapés*! Canapés are bite-sized executive nibbles to be offered around the room to your guests, ordinarily in a tasteful platter-type arrangement.

The canapé is versatile. A hungry businessman might require eleven or twelve popped into his hungry mouth after a hard day at the sharp end of office life. But just one or two is quite enough to satisfy the more restrained appetites of his waistline-conscious wife!

Canapés are tasty, adventurous and exotic. But most importantly of all they are stylish – served with flamboyance, flourish and – usually – some sort of sliced boiled egg adornment. Enjoy!

Sauerkraut Surprises

A surprise like the time you were invited over the road to Jean's house and she hadn't even mentioned that she'd just bought a brand new Magimix.

Mushroom Canapés

'It's ok Sandra. These only have 97 calories a pop.'

Stuffed Cocktail Grapes

'I'm telling you, Barry, you'd better get that promotion after the 3 hours I've spent stuffing these bloody grapes.'

Radish Bites

'Yes, I know you're watching your figure, Sandra, but I assure you there's only a smidge of cream cheese in them.'

Sardine Egg Canapés

'You're sure I can't tempt you with another, Mr Perkins?'

Ham Snacks

It really is as easy as wrapping some devilled ham in cream cheese. No, I don't know what devilled ham is either.

Goldfish Bowl

Such a fun way to serve oversized Wotsits.

Flavourful Seafood Dips

Come on in. The flavourful seafood dip is lovely.

Devilled Gherkin Eggs

The devil makes work for idle hands. But he also makes delicious stuffed eggs.

Worcester Beef Croûte

There is nothing like a bit of acupuncture to get my chi back in line.

Party
Cheese Ball

Monsieur, with these cheese balls you really are spoiling us.

Savoury
Edam Cheese

No, no Monsieur. No more cheese. Well, maybe just a sliver.

STARTERS

An autumn Saturday evening. Your guests, possibly your daughter's fiancé and his parents, are about to arrive. First impressions count so make sure your starters have been put out on display a good two to three hours in advance. I serve mine the continental way – chilled.

This gives you plenty of time to enjoy your Martini Bianco – and find out exactly what sort of family this Roger comes from.

Perfection Salad

Such unrealistic expectations upon the shoulders of young salads.

Potato Salad Log

This is no ordinary potato salad. This is a potato salad log.

Tomatoes Stuffed with Aubergine, Cream and Kiwi

'It's called a KIWI fruit Elaine. They come from China originally, you know.'

©The Sainsbury Archive, Museum of London

Stuffed Tomato Salad

That's it! Let it all hang out, love.

Hearty Corned Beef Salad

'Do you remember when Jane served us corned beef salad and it wasn't hearty in the slightest?'

Eggs Cooked Like Tripe

Side effects may include bloating, dizziness and hysteria.

Tomato Aspic

Ladies and Gentleman. I present the shoo-in for next year's Turner Prize.

Eggs in a Cage

For crimes against eggs, I sentence you to 7 years' hard labour.

Sandwich Loaf

To think the Earl of Sandwich died for this. . .

Celery Victor

To the victor belong the spoils.

Marinated Courgette Appetiser

'You'll never guess what the Americans call courgette Linda. . . Oh, you already knew.'

Party Sandwich Loaf

Run. Run as fast as you can. And whatever you do, don't look back.

Brawn with Strips of Pig's Ear

Apparently, this has a better flavour if you use a pickled pig's head, but a fresh one may be more convenient.

Veal Pâté with Calf's Brains

Crack open the Scotch. It's going to be a long night.

Emerald Cantaloupe

'Thank you, Jean. It *is* pretty, isn't it.'

Eggs in Aspic

How do you like your eggs in the morning? Oh. . .

Moulded Potato, Cheese and Pepper Salad

Once more unto the breach, dear friends.

Cucumber and Grape Mould

'Grapes, Jenny? I'm afraid they repeat on me something terrible.'

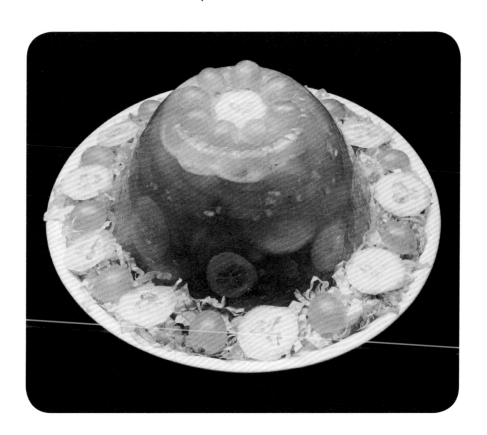

Prawn Stuffed
Tomatoes

We are not alone.

Party Ham Pâté

'I can't believe you haven't got a microwave yet, Claire.
I mean, who has time for an oven nowadays?'

Glazed Ham Loaf in a Ring

They came from the deep.

Spinach Ring

The valiant never taste of death but once.

MAIN COURSES

The main course is the main event. Whether it's a relaxed dinner with Bob and Sandra from next door or something more formal with your husband's boss and his beautiful but frosty wife, the main is what will make or break the evening.

Serve them something so visually compelling that hubby's pay-rise will be in the bag before they've even tasted the first mouthful. Remember, food is consumed as much by the eyes as the mouth.

Piquant Meat Loaf

Piquant – adj. having an agreeably pungent taste. I do so like pungent meat loaf.

Wurstel Sausage in Aspic

I predict 2017 will be the year of the suspended sausage.

Frankfurter Crown

The battle for Middle-Earth begins. . .

Seafood Mousse

Cheer up love, it might never happen.

Sausage-Stuffed Baked Marrow

How many eyes does horror have?

Cauliflower Loaf

'No, I'm not going to bloody well apologise, Digby.'

Macaroni, Ham and Cheese Bake

Crispy Cod Risotto

Taking the convenience out of convenience food.

Fish Sticks
with Pineapple

Fish Fingers. Too good to be wasted on the kids.

Sausage Savoury Salad

At least one of these words is correct.

Baked Stuffed Salmon

Excuse me mate, you've got something stuck in your teeth.

Fish Fingers À La King

This very same dish was served to George III on the occasion of his coronation.

Fish Whirls

'Prepare yourself for the most exciting, mesmerising and terrifying two hours of your life!'

Sausage Salad

Detox this, assholes!

Roast Suckling Pig Stuffed with Feta Cheese

Help me.

Wensleydale Marrow

It's. . . It's alive.

Fish Fingers in Foil

Now, there's posh.

Beefburger Pancakes

Beefier than Tom Hardy.

Macaroni Supper Casserole

You try cooking dinner for six after taking Mother to the chiropodist, picking Shelley up from tennis, *and* sewing on Johnny's Scouts' badges.

Hawaiian Baked Bean Casserole

Abandon hope all ye who enter here.

Hawaiian Frankfurter Platter

Imagine building a frankfurter tower so high that you could touch the clouds.

Cauliflower Surprise

Release the Kraken.

Turkey Loaf in Aspic

'Do stop snivelling, Timothy. *No one* likes radishes, but you're jolly well going to clean your plate.'

Curried Seafood in Pineapple Shells

I don't want to talk about this right now.

Suckling Pig with Sausage Meat and Apricot Stuffing

He who wishes to be obeyed must know how to command. . . Oh, sorry John. Didn't hear you come in.

Partridges with Orange and Vermouth Sauce

Oh this. . . It only took 6 hours. . . really no time at all.

The only thing we have to fear is fear itself.

Mushrooms
under Glass

So. Phis. Ti. Cated.

Sauced Pigeon's Breasts on Croutons

In case of emergency, please alert your nearest health practitioner.

Mussels and Cheese on Toast

Sweeeeeet Cheesus.

Maryland Chicken

Give me one good reason why you shouldn't eat chicken and bananas at the same time. One good reason.

Cherry Pineapple Bologna

The horrors these eyes have seen.

Ladies' Seafood Thermidor

'She really should have mentioned her allergy. . . Yes, I'm sure she'll be breathing perfectly normally come the morning.'

Shrimp-Salmon Mould

'I love you bro.' 'No, dude, I totally love you.'

Beefburger Cobbler

What is food to one man is bitter poison to another.

What's up, Doc?

SIDES

Your grandma served overcooked carrots and broccoli. Your mother served the same. But you're better than both of them. You are a sophisticated and modern woman with a firm grasp of continental culture and culinary *savoir faire* (Italian for style). That's why you put your veg in aspic whenever possible. After all, you wouldn't want Anita gossiping about your cauliflower, would you?

Celery Batons
in Pepper Rings

'Well, some of us need to watch our figure, Mary.'

Courgette Purée in Potato Baskets

I believe in France this is called *courgette purée en baskets de pommes de terre.*

Little Vegetable Towers

I like my spinach, mushrooms and broccoli like I like my men. Boiled, puréed and in a tower.

Carrot Ring with Peas

'I do think it's clever how this matches your curtains, Diane.'

Split Pea Whip

This is your brain, on drugs.

Broccoli Tower

Spare a thought for the humble cauliflower; always the bridesmaid. . .

Purée of Peas in Pastry Barquettes

'Another barquette, Deirdre?'

Orange Baskets

Turns out oranges *are* the only fruit.

Italian Bananas

'Darling, tell them about that divine trattoria they simply *must* visit next time they're in Rome.'

Almond and Black Cherry Aspic Salad

65 million years in the making.

AROUND THE WORLD

There are just some guests that you need to pull out all the stops for. Your husband's boss, for example. Promotions don't just happen. They need to be earned. And who better to promote to Regional Sales Manager for the South-West than the man who is cultured and *au fait* with the finer things in life. *Au fait?* Why, that's just in the know in French.

Creamed Eggs on Fried Noodles

It's not *exactly* the same as the one at the Golden Dragon, but they only had Pot Noodle at The Co-op.

Zulu Beef Stew

Sliced bananas just add such an authentic twist, don't you think?

Eggs en Gelée

It seems we've entered the seventh circle of hell.

French Aubergine Mould

You were warned never to push Carrie to the limit. Now you must face the evil consequences.

Chaud-froid of Chicken

They'd never forget the day Maureen attempted the Chaud-froid.

Chicken Chaud-froid

Once you stop screaming, then you'll start talking about it.

Mousse de Volaille à L'Indienne

Well, I know you could get a takeaway, but I just think it's so much *nicer* to make it yourself.

Mousse de Saumon

Guaranteed to impress even the snootiest members of your bridge club.

Veau Farci en Gelée

Even the French don't know what this is.

Salmon Pudding (Lachspudding)

Serve it with piped mayonnaise and olives. Or don't. I'm sure it will be delicious either way.

Veal Élégante

I do so love French cuisine. It's just so refined.

DESSERTS

Many a wobbly dinner party can be redeemed at the final hurdle with a cracking dessert. Banish painful memories of undercooked chicken, dowdy carrots (or that upsetting conversation your husband started about James Callaghan's socialist government) with a knock-out finale that is sexy, sweet and stylish. Why not push the boat out and serve it with a dessert wine such as Babycham or Grand Marnier?

Apricot Creams

Are you eating it? Or is it eating you?

Tasty Tofu-Rice Pudding

Even those peculiar vegetarian 'friends' of your son would enjoy this tasty treat.

Prune Whip

'And what's more, Sally, it helps keep you regular. . .'

Tasty Tofu-Rice Pudding

Even those peculiar vegetarian 'friends' of your son would enjoy this tasty treat.

Jellied 'Peach Melba'

Cheetah sold separately.

Party Mushrooms

In my day, 'party mushrooms' were something else altogether.

Prune Whip

'And what's more, Sally, it helps keep you regular. . .'

Flaming Baked Apples

'Do be careful with those matches, Duncan. Remember what happened with the camping stove in Brittany.'

Blue Cheese Ball

Even mousey can't resist such a treat.

Cheese 'Pineapple'

'You are clever, Peggy. It looks just like a real pineapple. No, none for me thanks.'

CAKES

Everyone loves cake, don't they? But anyone can make a Victoria sponge. And if your coffee morning is going to be considerably more interesting than last week's one at Deborah's, your cake needs to be iced to buggery. For a classy twist, add lavish amounts of alcohol to your cake mix. Sherry, Bailey's or, at a stretch, even a bottle or two of hubby's light ale will add a real zing to your bake.

Teddy Bear Cake

The ultimate battle. Bear vs Bear. There can be only one winner.

Zundy Teddy Bear Cake

(My money's on Zundy.)

Kevin Kitten

Little would you suspect that Kevin's just disembowelled a mouse.

Hedgehog Cake

The name *hedgehog* is derived from the Middle English *heyghoge*, from *heyg*, because it frequents hedgerows, and *hogge* from its piglike snout.

Fondant Icing
Clown Cake

Good night sweet prince.

Pousse Café Gateau

50% rainbow + 50% booze = 100% cake

FESTIVE

Jingle-jangle! Are those Santa's sleigh bells you hear? Well, then it's time to lend some yuletide cheer to your culinary stylings. The Dawsons at Number 72 might think they've trumped you with that, quite frankly, vulgar tree they mounted onto the pebble dash, but Gary and Barb won't be feeling quite so pleased with themselves when they see the amount of spray-painted holly you've used to adorn your Christmas nibble platter.

Father
Christmas Cake

Give us a smile, darlin'.

Christmas Popcorn Balls

Guaranteed to cheer up even the grumpiest Santa.

An Old-Fashioned Bell and Festive Apricot Ornament

There is simply no need to spend lots of money on fancy lights and tinsel.

Gala Fruit Mould

'Tis the season to be jelly.

Gelatin Christmas Trees

'Look, kids. Santa's been extra generous with the parsley this year.'

Snowmen
Meringues

Now fellas, play nice. We don't want any trouble here.

Festive Chicken Salad Log

Deck the halls with boughs of holly. And sesame seeds, onion, olives and pimento.

Apricot Carolling Tree

The perfect edible present for Auntie Gail.

MORNING AFTER

It's just as well you made up the spare room. Eight bottles of Liebfraumilch and a bottle of Mateus Rosé really do slip down quite easily, don't they? But now you're faced with *the breakfast dilemma*. Cornflakes just won't do. But these rather more swishy morning dishes can be whipped up in no time at all. Serve your frankfurter soup with a side dish of Aspirin and that crippling hangover will soon be a distant memory.

Ham and Bananas Hollandaise

Ham? Check. Bananas? Check. Hollandaise? Check. And you're good to go.

British Brunch Fondue

Ladies and Gentlemen! I present THE ULTIMATE HANGOVER CURE!

Breakfast Brightener Soup

Kill or cure time, Trevor.

Eggs Guacamole

Yo, hipsters! **This** is what eggs and avocado should look like.

FOR THE KIDS

Why shouldn't children be preparing food as visually hypnotic as my perfect Croûte aux Morilles? Why should they be expected to make the best of a grim, unset Butterscotch Angel Delight while Mum finesses her latest dazzling gastronomic creation? Do not deprive your little ones. They are, after all, the dinner party hosts and hostesses of the future. Start them on an ice cream clown. Kids love clowns.

And what do you *do* for a living?

Be a Clown Party

By blood a king, in heart a clown.

Paper
Bag Party

All work and no play makes Jack a dull boy.

Viking Jellies

Hail Thor, son of Odin, father of Modi, Magni and Thrud.

Edible Clowns

The Carrot Girls

The darkest places in hell are reserved for those who maintain their neutrality in times of moral crisis.

GIVE IT A GO

You have been shown the wonders of the '70s dinner party. Now, if you've been paying close attention, you will be ready to host your own. Here are six classic recipes to whet the appetite. Why not give them a go? And do report back @70s_party.

FIVE-CAN CASSEROLE

1 can mushroom soup
1 can chicken soup
1 small can evaporated milk
1 can chow mein noodles
1 can chicken
1 clove garlic, finely chopped
1 packet ready salted crisps, crushed

Mix the first 6 ingredients together in a large bowl, place in an ovenproof dish and sprinkle the crushed crisps on top. Bake for an hour at 175°C/ 350°F.

(Inspired by Mrs Wallace W. Morse)

HOT DOG SURPRISE #1

6 hot dogs
1 x 275g (10 oz) can cream of
celery soup
225g (8 oz) cream cheese at room temperature
36 melba toast rounds
36 sprigs of parsley

Finely chop the hot dogs until the texture of mince, then in a bowl mix well with the cream cheese and celery soup. Leave for 1 hour in the fridge to set. Spread the mixture on top of the melba toast rounds and grill until the top is a pale golden brown. Garnish with the parsley sprigs and serve immediately.

(Inspired by *The Cook's Treasury* by Betty Brown)

Beef Tingler

2 large tins condensed beef broth
2 large tins water
¼ cup brandy
¼ cup whipping cream

¼ teaspoon vanilla extract
Pinch of nutmeg
Pinch of cinnamon
¼ teaspoon grated orange rind

Mix together the beef broth, water and brandy in a saucepan and gently heat, stirring occasionally and making sure the mixture doesn't boil. Combine the cream, vanilla, nutmeg and cinnamon together in a bowl and beat until the cream forms peaks. Carefully stir in the orange rind and serve on top of the warmed soup.

(Inspired by *Ideals Christmas Cookbook Treasury*)

SMOKED BEEF DIP

---

1 teaspoon minced onion
1 tablespoon sherry
225g (8 oz) cream cheese
2 tablespoons mayonnaise
8 stuffed olives, minced
75g (3 oz) smoked beef, minced
1 teaspoon paprika

In a bowl, soak the minced onion in the sherry until soft.
Add all the remaining ingredients and mix well.
Serve with a selection of crudités.

(Inspired by Mrs Roger C. Wilder)

HOT DOG SURPRISE #2

6 hot dogs
275g (10 oz) tin tomato soup
1 cup grated mature cheddar
1 teaspoon horseradish
1 teaspoon mustard
24 olives, halved
48 cocktail crackers

Finely chop the hot dogs, place in a bowl and then add the tomato soup, cheese, horseradish and mustard. Mix to combine well and then spread the mixture over the crackers. Place on a baking tray and grill until they're a light shade of brown. Top with half an olive and serve immediately.

(Inspired by *The Cook's Treasury* by Betty Brown)

GRAPE WINE

450g (16 oz) frozen grape juice
50g (2 oz) frozen apple juice
1 cup sugar
1 teaspoon dry yeast

Mix all the ingredients together in a bowl and stir until dissolved. Pour into a 5 litre (1 gallon) flask and then fill with water to just below the top. Stretch a large balloon over the mouth of the flask and secure it with a rubber band. Leave to ferment for 3 weeks before decanting.

(Inspired by Gertrude Hogate)

PHOTOGRAPHY CREDITS

10 Good Housekeeping Children's Cookbook, Ebury; 20, 31, 33, 38, 44, 56, 57, 60, 62, 64, 104, 114 Recipe Cards Curtin Publications Inc., NYC; 16, 21, 23, 26, 34, 39, 41, 85, 86, 142, 147, 148, 154, 155, 156, Betty Crocker Recipe Cards, used with permission of General Mills Marketing Inc.; 27, 30, 36, 50, 72, 73, 106, 122, 123, 137, 146 originally published in McCall's® Great American Recipe Cards; 17, 19, 74, 76, 77, 87, 96, 119, 120, Weight Watchers Diet Cards, 1974 and 1982; 18, 22, 24, 35, 37, 40, 42, 45, 46, 58, 59, 65, 70, 92, 93, 94, 95, 97, 98, 107, 108, 113, 121, 125, 131, 132, 149 *Carrier's Kitchen* by Robert Carrier; 25, 43, 47, 51, 54, 55, 68, 69, 78, 79, 80, 84, 89, 99, 100, 101, 105, 109, 111, 129, 133 Supercook Magazines – *The Encyclopedia of World Cooking*; 32 *Festive Food And Party Pieces* by Josceline Dimbleby,1982 ©The Sainsbury Archive, Museum of London; 48, 49 *The Book of Microwave Cookery* by Sonia Allison, 1980 edition; 61, 63, 71, 75, 88 Birds Eye Recipe Cards; 66, 67 *Every Day Cook Book* by Marguerite Patten, 1968; 81, 82, 118, 152, 153, 158, 159 F*anny and Johnnie Cradock Cookery Programme* © Michael Leale; 83 *The Party Cookbook* by Annette Wolter, 1974; 110, 112 *Cordon Bleu Cookery Course*, 1976/77 © Mike Leale; 124, 138, 139, 140, 143 *Ideals Christmas Cookbook Treasury* by Naomi Arbit and June Turner, 1975 & 1978; 128, 130, 136 *Cake Icing And Decorating*, St Michael Cookery Library, 1978 © Barry Bullough; 141, 157 Images from *A Ladybird Cookery Book: Party Food* © Ladybird Books Ltd, 1982.

Every effort has been made to trace or contact copyright holders. The publishers will be pleased to make good any omissions or rectify any mistakes brought to their attention at the earliest opportunity.

ACKNOWLEDGEMENTS

The 70s dinner party stemmed of course from the 60s dinner party, and continued through the early 80s. For this reason, some of the photos included in this book are from the decades either side of the 70s.

I was helped with this project by many people but first, I have to thank the photographers and companies who allowed me to use their pictures – especially Mike Leale and Barry Bullough.

Big thanks to my friend and agent, Becky Thomas. It would make her very uncomfortable if I said anything too nice, but she has been brilliant.

Then, of course, everyone at Square Peg – chiefly Rosemary Davidson and Susannah Otter. Thank you for the guidance, the help and the general encouragement. And thanks also to James Ward, Rowena Skelton-Wallace, Alison Tulett, Lisa Fiske, Kate Neilan, Jane Kirby, Penny Liechti, Lisa Gooding and Mari Yamazaki.

To the superhuman Clare Bowes for making the whole thing 100x easier.

To Carly Rogers of Carly Rogers Flowers (and her glamorous assistant, Alex) – you're a wonderful human being and maybe an even more wonderful florist.

To Linda, Jake ~~and Tom Pallai~~ – thank you for the cookbooks and endless hot dog recipes.

To Mopsy, for buying up Ebay's recipe card collection.

To Sue, for the tablecloths and napkins. I'm only sorry I couldn't find a use for the Christmas Pudding tea-cosy.

To Mum. Thanks for the cookbooks, the photos, the use of your eggcups, the childcare, hemming my skirt even though it was really wonky, the tablecloths, the tea. . . Oh, and everything else you've done and continue to do.

To Dad. Thanks for everything, including the meatloaf and stuffed peppers. They made me the (vegetarian) woman I am today.

To Bren, the best Mother-in-Law I could hope for.

To Baz, for saying you'd never buy this, let alone look at it.

To Coco, the best girl in the world and my twinnie forever. I love you very very much and always will.

To Lenny, the best boy in the world. I love you very very much too – you're a superstar.

To Nelson. You're an idiot.

And thanks to everyone else who donated books, recipes and pictures.

And, finally, to Sam. I'm sorry I got a book deal. But it's all your fault. You shouldn't have been so nice to me these past 20 years. And you certainly shouldn't have helped me at all with this. I love you very very much – you're the greatest.

ABOUT THE AUTHOR

Anna Pallai is a PR and agent and formerly Publicity Director at Faber where she helped manage the publishing careers of Harry Hill, Ricky Gervais, Richard Ayoade, David Mitchell and numerous others. She was born midway through the 1970s and vividly recalls the period of 1975-80 as being a personal culinary nadir. Having been forcefed devilled eggs, stuffed peppers and Hungarian meat stews of dubious origin from birth, she went vegetarian aged twelve and hasn't looked back since.